Praise for *topography of a border / line bird*

Juania Sueños's fragmented prose glitters across her debut collection, *topography of a border / line bird*, detailing memories of her and her family's complicated experiences in the U.S. Her poems are donned in black velvet, whispering truths and obsessions to an altar of Mexican ancestors. Sueños constellates familial love and trauma, past relationships, queer precolonial history, and the realities that haunt and harm immigrants in Texas. Sueños's speaker pulls apart the language imposed upon her by therapists, family, and the state, and births this incredible book of poetry.

—**Cloud Delfina Cardona**, author of *What Remains* and *the past is a jean jacket*

These poems sing, offering small narrative treasures that rumble through Juania's throat. Capable of surprise, desire, longing, and justice too. Traveling through these pages, they embrace and craft beauty in a time and space when it's most needed.

—**jo reyes-boitel**, poet and playwright, author of *the matchstick litanies*

Tender, inventive, and brilliant—Juania Sueños' poems are punk rock. These poems are charged with grief for family, history, and dare readers to reflect on hard truths. Her work reflects on the intimate connections between family and history: "before I remember / I must work / from memory." Through artifacts, erasure, and photographs, Sueños celebrates the topographies of a border shaped by a desire that makes immigrants want to dance like "confetti against gray skies" because home feels impossible in a country where love songs aren't simply love songs. These poems love and lament the restless nature of life with extreme abandon. They depart and transgress what it means to name a place heaven. Each poem is an event worth celebrating because even when the "earth hurts," a bright star is possible. Shatter your heart with this debut!

—**Sebastian Páramo**, author of *Portrait of Us Burning*

In *topography of a border / line bird*, Juania Sueños traces dreamlike cartography of a life formed by migration, queerness, survival, and ancestral summoning. These poems challenge lineage, expose the harsh immigration policies, face matriarchs, and grief through enticing forms, tender yet aching language that sings through pages. Through this honest collection, rooted in the voice of a daughter, undocumented migrant, and fierce granddaughter, Sueños reclaims her place in the archive—not through permission, but through fire, prayer, and poetry.

—**Saúl Hernández**, author of *How to Kill a Goat & Other Monsters*

topography of a border / line bird

Juania Sueños

MOUTHFEEL PRESS

Contents

The exile feels that the state of exile has the structure of a dream.

—Dubravka Ugrešić

If I go ahead with my fragmentary visions, the whole world will have to be transformed in order for me to fit within it.

—Clarice Lispector

Como buena Mexicana, sufriré el dolor tranquila.

—Lucha Villa

¡Chanfles!

—Chespirito

For my Abue Carolina & the women in my family who spread wings
into the unknown   split their minds.

Border / Line Bird

Departation

Dear Doghouse

let me fall in love   with those murdered

their names   I can't remember

now

I'll replace them with

     your
         name

whisper it in phone calls

     across rivers

this ancient poem

     sí, quizás tendremos hijos

güeritos algún día, tía.

it always happens this way after

the thieves leave   we search

     for what their hands hold

like fiends, tiptoeing
around a big-

     windowed house

I upholster the walls with

     mirrors

so I can see you   parched god

enter me   close-eyed   I beg for

     blows

destruction maybe…in my native

     lengua

     the dirtier one

I've always been good at   reassurance

I am who you say I am

                                                                     sucia

                                                                     loca

                                                                     perra

an old trope

Lucy the ejected

on fire   engulfed in sick   desire victim

of your superiority

carried in blood   Yes you too bleed

you too

                                                   stain with dark

I   little i   have learned

hatred between blood   lines   god   mortal

chinga'o the luck of the draw!

every morning

when i watch the news   i kneel

                                          i offer my flor y canto

allegiance to Him (you?)

my dear   Doghouse   i can't even say

                                        your name

but here is another

                              poem   (this is only a poem!)

                        sweet baby after you
come i light
                                                        candles for the shrine

i climb   your mountain

                                                        yerbaniz

            of my ancestors
                                        in my pockets

i struggle to erect

                        a church for you   your own Tepeyac

                        i wait undressed

 for you to imprint   your image

                                                        on my body

but you're watching
                                        white

women fuck   on a cracked phone   could you hear me

                        translate

Audre Lorde   to my mother

            In the recognition of   *loving lies*

                        an answer
                                        to desperation

she too loves   you   all of you when you vote democrat

when you threaten to call

                  I.C.E.
   i'm well aware of why we

                    love
              canela
cominos

                   serranos

                  chile de árbol

sanded boiling   deserts   bailes

mezcal
      rancheras   cumbia   circles
         sweat
glimmering   stars under

      strobe lights   you

you remember when   we forget
                to fill our cups
       with melted gold
  we drink   slowly

pero de algo
       nos vamos   a morir
   dear
        Doghouse
    neither of us can   say the words

      we want to say   (¡ja! drew my little
blade

toward the sky)

                                        departed

de-partition

                                                a split

            celebration

My Daughter Is What You Think

Bonita, brillante, but you should know
she's *explosiva*, same as the women in our family, myself included.

My mother gave this disclaimer
to the man who wanted to marry me.

Bonita, brillante, explosiva
sky-fire before the blankness of night—a lack of vision.

I need an unreasonable amount of time alone.
My time of purge, like a Lent spring.

At a coffee shop, my friend tells me she prefers lunatic from the list
of words invented to describe the condition of being apt for disclaimers

Neurotic sounds too Woody Allen. We laugh then walk to a botánica
where I contemplate buying anything that claims cleansing.

I can't remember when the explosions started. But I know
the first time I wished to die, I was tucked into a pink

bed while my mother's wails echoed through the walls of my room.
I pressed a pillow on my face until it hurt.

Yesterday, the dog fished a tuna can from the recycle bin. She licked the thin
blade until her tongue and paws bloodied the carpet.

Maybe it's easier—licking wounds than eluding sharp objects,
The way it's easier to pull knife to throat in exchange for love.

Every therapist, psychiatrist, every lover has come up with a new

name for me. I call it collapsing to the capital sin of wrath. La *ira*, passing train,
shattering windows of every home I've made.

I've always loved trains—their warning horn, their rattling rusted metal,
the way they can send the great blue heron flying.

Who will clean your toilets?

I kept hearing

a question indicative of what's always been.
What value can we materialize? We the ones

who make life tidier–shiny. We the people
who cycle on the wheels of capital

bags of cement in an empty
lot transformed into student housing or a new

suburb soon filled with children
on bikes, elephant ears, birds

of paradise in yards.

What is it? this argument—someone's inconvenience
vs our mother, our sister, our best friend, our uncle.

Most of my life, I felt a fissure every time. . .
a breakage. My little basin spilled water

on my lap. Nothing is above toilets, carpets, marbled floors, granite counters,
lunch specials—here, we live en la superficie.

I'm no longer appalled—
at diseases, plagues, drugs, or rapists (ha! this is even more ironic now).

It used to make me sad when I saw you baseball-capped,
chalked boots with fly ash and lime, bandanas hiding

a sigh of exhaustion

but maybe it was a smile. In deadly weather
there were men whistling, perched on roofs like birds

Pinche enamorado play something else
not my father's music—cumbia, algo movido

maybe we were always making

      beauty

when the trees were bare I saw you making their leaves—
maroons and oranges—dance in the wind

confetti against gray skies.

No Mexicans Were Hung on This Tree

While on a birthday road trip in Goliad, Texas, we stop in the middle of the historic
downtown beneath a massive tree
there is a plaque reassuring us that it was not used to hang Mexicans

The book i checked out from the library says otherwise about the tree & its uses
i am also Mexican & that is a strength i suppose
like the Mexican carters who traded goods & were presumably good men
the white Texans frequently raided them on their paths ambushing them at night
i see their limp bodies hanging from trees on my walk back to camp & repeat
the plaque's words before falling asleep

TEXAS
THE HANGING TREE

Rose Tattoos

your love was Pinback
& Conway Twitty & DEVO
migas & blueberry pancakes, the roses &
thorns you etched on my thigh, on my elbow

two months after my grandmother's death

   love was begging the Heavens
   to let me keep you & your lanky hands
   around my throat
   your red round eyes   bells ringing
   my windless pipes
   my shrinking lungs

   your sweet nothin's *i'm gonna fucking kill you*

     go back to Mexico, ugly bitch

        go back. . .
         go back. . .

love was my joy at the irony
of Mexicans shoving you handcuffed into the SUV
that drove you down a dark gravel road

love became the sunset glow
of nightmares
its windchimes of rape
its gun's grainy-spark

   its blunted crystal stabbings
   its version of me & my wrath ramming
   a weedwacker through the stomach of a man
   the song of tearing flesh
   the beauty of shredded
   organs sifting down like snowflakes
   on my shoulders

love is seeing roses on my skin
& remembering pleading
for the bounce of the needle

Now That You Are Dead

your sister-in-law
Mariquita has not died
at 96 she cries
                              when I speak your name & I smile
for as long as I can before

worrying I'm selfishly
keeping you in this place
                              are you really here?
when I try I don't believe
you are the red   lantana beneath my feet
                             you're memories that visit

depending on my mood
a happy one of you singing
on your birthday   when the sky's clear

on this day you're   the story Mariquita tells
of pink slips of paper
from the telephone company
a jar filled with proof of another

                                          betrayal from Abuelito
you were quick to throw
                             a match in the glass & burn the love notes
without reading   you watched the ashes fall
they reminded you of   the first time
                                     you saw snow & you knew
white fields hardly ever happen
                             he's not always this bad
you had to say this like a prayer
                             as if the snow was a miracle
you repeated this like you are
                             all that is good & preserved
                                          through blood

your pain as told by the ridges
& folds of your old friend's earthly flesh
ripples of ocean separate her from me
                              but she too sees the dead
you in a dream

                              by the old Ford waving

you say   *vamonos a dar una vuelta*
Not now, she says

Antes de que nos olviden

> "Haremos historia
> No andaremos de rodillas"
>
> —Caifanes

After Neruda's "La Memoria"

para usted, a'pa

It's a recent thing, this memory—

of my father in a straw hat sitting beneath
a peach tree—his gaze distant & steeped in quiet

pride. He digs for his swiss army knife in his shirt's breast pocket
& splits the red flesh from the marrow-white of an apple

or did he slice up the fruit & eat it one piece at a time?
or did the knife wait in the leather sheath of his belt?

Father, forgive me for not remembering you well
for when you see me eating an apple skin & all

I Catch & Release the News

*a former prison warden & his brother face additional charges in the shooting
of migrants in west texas. . .the victims were not identified by name.—CNN*

they call it that as if we are fish. born to blue vastness caught by nets or state lines.
toss that which is not useful. in rich countries, fishing is a sport. i am told they catch
then release the fish as if the entire point is power, a tally that is fun & bottomless.
freedom is an ability to float in sweet or brackish waters. imagine a sailor who does
not belong at sea. imagine jesus of nazareth on a raft, net in hand. predicting an
animalness, they want me to bite *anzuelos suelo* the granular ground hooking my
annular mouth pariah mouthing. baiting when you present what is not presentable.
i am numb, no longer knocked to my knees, pierced by hooks & tv news & border
budgets. when i reach for the sky, water pours from my body. what is the difference
between releasing & controlling? think of the reservoir he last drank from. what is
the difference between a hog a bird & a duck? the Sheppard brothers learned while
hunting: there is no difference. fish hog bird duck man woman drinking life. *come out
you sons of bitches, little asses.* the same corrugated-eyed warden who some time ago
spoke sweet words a father tells his son, *now you belong to me, boy*[1]

[1]https://law.utexas.edu/wp-content/uploads/sites/11/2018/03/2018-03-IC-WTDF-Report.pdf

The Immigrants, They Want to Dance All Night Long

after The Clash "Straight to Hell"

There ain't no need for you
they told you, tío,
but look at your yellow house
your shirts still hanging in that closet
you'd just built a shoe rack
for your favorite pairs of Doc Martens
you could have these earthly treasures safely
shipped right to the steps of your new home—
but waiting is a better gift
with its element of unknowing—
what surprise could the universe
or the U.S. hold for you this time?
you now live near clouds
on the highest peaks of Monterrey. . .
San Pedro—building a golden temple on a stone
but even the key to the Heavens couldn't unlock
the silver shackles adorning your ankles
when you walked out, our mother gasped
her eyes wide, hands on her lap
gripping one another. she did not speak
on the flight back

You're shaking
your head now. this is an old
story. I know
what you're thinking:

Have your husband the activist help
us return to that night dream
your silver hair shining over chilaquiles
I wonder about your illegitimate child
—how all transgressions evaporate when
tragedy strikes. you were only human
with a *free ride* back to where they
always tell us to go back to—
                              home

except there was no home
except home was a shared toilet in a room
with a dozen others
except home was a white room
no windows no mates no food no light
no words no world no wife no child
no father no mother

home: an immaculate
silence of pain   uttered as *let me out*
but that too passed

Today is a new
celebration, a birthday with a live
band and too many bottles of tequila
margaritas on the rocks like your mother
cuba libres like your father
shame does not penetrate this place
after all. your american dream carried
you to a new status back to this mother
land and this palace passed as a house
and the 50k spent on a quinceañera
so they stop calling your daughter *pocha*
we dance at the party until promises
of sobriety plunge into the pools and
cell phones ruined drowned our disappointment
the night sky soaks up your tears
I'm afraid you'll fall out of this truck
your head barely makes it to my lap
Did you see? They gave her a diamond.
¡Nos aceptan! Nos aceptan, Lin

I'm Suckered Into Paying JSTOR Forty Bucks for *Faggots & Sodomites Lesbians & Hermaphrodites*

determined to find out once & for all if my queer ancestors were also as neurodivergent funny & had great taste in music   paraphrasing:

Patlachui *a filthy woman a woman with a penis   possessor of an erect penis   a penis & testicles   pairs up with a woman befriends a woman procures young women & possesses young women   the top part of the patlache's body is that of a man   she talks like a man & passes him or herself off as a man   has a beard body hair   does it to another woman [tepatlachuia]   befriends a woman never wants to marry   detests & never looks at men they're frightening   she is frightening to look at also   from the stem patlach a wide thing defined   in colonial dictionaries as for one woman to do it with another*[2]

Xochihua *although Anderson & Dibble translated it as pervert   it literally means flower bearer   a cross-dressing person who performs various functions of women   the flower is a vital metaphor   in the Nahua universe it's used to denote philosophy poetry & song   a general symbol of life's dualities.*[3]

abuelito often reprimanded my mother *don't hug him too much he might turn jotolingo* when she embraced her son *joto*   fag   *lingo*   a dialect   form of expression display of the feminine what he meant to say was *don't turn him into a woman weak a target*

below there is a man on fire   they call him *puto priest* they burn him because he behaves like a woman   they lied singed life for propagandist means the *Mexicas* had used for queers like a spoon or a fork   no reason for arson

> sexual conquest
>
> a modification of how a savage performs
>
> coco as in head as in lava
>
> pouring or purifying from the Spanish lavar
>
> washing
>
> hogs
>
> lava-coco
>
> the beautiful the colonial
>
> the liquid contents filling
>
> scorched rock

[2–3]Pete Sigal Queer Nahuatl Sahagún's *Faggots & Sodomites Lesbians & Hermaphrodites Ethnohistory*, 1 January 2007.

Pete Sigal
22

Abuelisa Has Been Watching *Orange is the New Black*

1. The smell of wet soil trickles inside Abuelisa's house. Her gaze lingers on the rose bush before entering, illuminated by the full moon. Her large Mexican pink petals match the house's door and trimming. They've grown so wild that they're obstructing the doorway, despite the freeze and lack of care. She hasn't been in the U.S. in months, or maybe a year. *Esta muy solita Lindita, por eso viné*, she tells me, leaning on the kitchen island. The next few weeks she'll care for me like I'm dying of cancer. Every morning I smell papitas con chile and café de olla before 9 AM. Today, she goes into my room to make my bed even though I've told her repeatedly not to. *I'll do it, Abuelisa, descanse.* I leave my plate and walk over to stop her, but as I approach the hallway, I see her shake the sheets and a photo strip flutters out slowly, landing on the mattress.

2. In the first photo, your shoulder touches mine beneath Rio Luna, the horchateria in Long Beach. We took the blue line metro rail there. *That line is dangerous. Let's take an Uber*, you said, but I didn't hear you, as I often didn't in my I'm older (and muy, muy taller) arrogance, always infantilizing you. When we get off the metro, I see a man creep out of the passenger window of an old Camaro, pointing a gun at the pedestrians waiting to cross, shoot and slide back into the car as quickly as a clown bursts out of a crank box. A figure collapses on the sidewalk. The car peels off. An older woman screams, calling out for help, and I dramatically tackle you to the ground, dragging you behind the station's ticket booth. This cheap *American Gangster* episode however doesn't stop us from quickly laughing the entire way to the beach. When we make it to the horchateria, we're so high on sunlight and the thrill of having survived a "shooting," we call it, but we both mean, *survive*, period. Make it another day without being found out by your family, or mine. In the second photo on the film strip (I paid five dollars for, as I always paid, taking on the role of a man taking care of you. Talk about a high! The high of power, of pride of successful protection!). Your hair is black, smooth, cut like a school boy's. I'm in a denim long-sleeve shirt, pearl-snaps buttoned to my neck. Your nose to my ear asking for a kiss, but I look straight ahead, staring at myself, wondering how long it'll take before I snap out of this sin, or how long until my punishment comes.

3. Abuelisa lowers the pillow she was fluffing. She's been watching *Orange is the New Black*, wide-eyed when Piper and Alex finally make out after many episodes, *¿Con una mujer?* She says, gasping. I go to bed wondering if she'll drop the show, but the next evening she asks me to put it on for her, and we watch the romance unfold together.

4. In the third photo, a longer piece of black hair swings below the split of your chin. I think, ok, people who ask us if we're sisters have a point, same skin tone, same thick dark hair. You look like a child who's just gotten compliments from her parents in that baggy, brown pea coat you got from the thrift store down the street from your house, the one you shared with two generations. Punk parents born and raised in East L.A., smoking pot in the house during the day, and camping in Nevada at night. They didn't care to make money. And your grandparents—from a small town outside Mexico City—too tired for *we raised you better*s. Working six days a week until dark, fixing cars, cleaning offices. I envied you and the way time and love felt abundant there. You're grabbing my face, pinching my cheeks together, making me look like a fish, as if you knew I'd left the booth, as if you knew I went to that place to the pool of guilt and needed you to pull me out.

5. I try moving forward as quietly as I can, watching Abuelisa tuck the sheets under the mattress and put the photo back on the nightstand. Your plane will land before noon and I feel a rush of dread at the thought of us sharing a bed next to Abuelisa's room. Your flight is delayed, of course, and I smoke a few cigarettes, waiting in the parking lot calling tías, *Are you staying at grandma's? Yes,* Lucero and Chata say. As soon as you open the car door, I yell at you to book a hotel. Tonight, more primos, tías, tíos, and the tíos' and tías' moms will be in town from Mexico for a baptism. They've come to stay at the house and I can't fathom explaining our relationship, lying unsuccessfully since they expected this when I cut my hair short and started posting photos of us on Instagram. I don't speak to you on the drive from the airport to the only motel we can afford. Everything you do bothers me. *Shut off that fucking music, Ani.*

6. The motel air feels old and damp like someone has relentlessly smoked there night after night. I cry into the dimple of your clavicle, *I'm sorry. It's not you I'm mad at. It never is,* you say, then start to brag about the birthmark below it. *It's a fresa,* you say this each time, and each time I fall into the trap by caressing it with my fingers.

7. An hour before the party, I fixate on my hair and eventually ask you to shave a V on the back of my head with a razor, which you say is a bad idea, and you're right—it only makes me feel worse afterward. Between cake icing and margaritas and pink tulle on the tables, people ask me what I did to my hair.

No sé. I introduce you as Anais, no title. We dance together for one song until I can't stand the stares. Suddenly I feel a rush of adrenaline, and decide I want to be this badass, this no-bullshit cabrona, someone who views outsiders with no interest in pleasing or acknowledging them, except as a possible punching bag if they dare insult, or look at us feo. I wave sarcastically at a woman in a beige sequin dress leaning on the open bar who's been looking at us the entire song. I want to be the opposite of what everyone told me I was. Sensitive, weak.

8. Nobody asks how we know each other, and we leave early by boarding my Abuelisa's van. I drive home and let you hold my hand even though I know everyone on board can see us each time a car nears with amber lights.

9. It's my mom's restaurant's Christmas party. A week has passed since the baptism. You've been here since then. My Abuelisa made me swear I'd never leave my room to go to a hotel again, so we shared my bed. I still don't touch you. Each time you come near me, something heavy strikes my chest like I've actually been shot (and not because of the blue line!) In the mornings, my Abuelisa tries to make conversation, but you're the sweet, mute chaparrita in flats, and that's who you've become around most Texans. Not tonight, everybody's dancing, drinking palomas, and we sing The Smiths, *I wonder to myself: Could life ever be sane again?* My mother takes a photo of us in front of the mural we painted on the wall adjacent to the tortilla machine, an anatomical heart with veins sprawling, piercing through the red dirt in a cornfield. It took us three days to finish—your strokes, slow and trembly. A man came in agitated and yelled, *What are you scared of? Don't be scared! Just paint it!* Why were we scared, *Ani?*

10. My Abuelisa sips her margarita and bobs her head to the music. She pauses and pulls out a small pink box from her purse. A set of Victoria's Secret lip glosses. You don't wear lip gloss, but you say *Muchas gracias señora,* four or five times with reddened eyes. She nods slowly. *I hope you like them.* I give her a big kiss on her temple, and we keep on singing until everyone goes home.

I changed my name

to Leonarda, swapped the *o* from Leonardo
to confirm I was now your daughter
you were my first step
father. This made the family laugh,
and you flashed that cool smile.
Your mustard, snake-skin boots
a beam of charm in the room and
a belt to match.

At school everyone said you looked so young,
que guapo. I was proud.
Some evenings you put on
expensive cologne just to drive
me around in your blue truck
changing Bobby Pulido's song
to a joke *voy de pelado*,
shameless. And you weren't joking.

Ma told me you bought the truck
with money taken from the drawer
of the tortilleria where you didn't show
up. She pulled her hair
turning llantos to maldiciones,
watching tortillas fall on the floor
along with her dreams
of a family.

Sometimes I ask her what's become
of you. He is an alcoholic. Never stopped.
Pray for him. Instead I remember the red
plastic jeep you sent one Christmas,
how excited I was to show it off
and say it came from *La Planta*,
I misheard Atlanta, so every time I rode
around the plaza, I imagined you
like the little boy climbing up a big
stalk only to find a curt giant
blocking the entrance to the skies.

I must confess, sometimes you are
a character in my novel,
rastros de un rostro,
an unfinished portrait
filled in by one-sided details.
Though most days, I don't think of you,
except when my windows are down,
one hand on the wheel
the other dancing in the wind
my voice singing *voy desvelado.*

At the House of the First Mexican Woman Muralist, Aurora Reyes

Under the sky's strawberry smear
my son & I lean on the naked brick parapet shaded by violet jacarandas.

Inside are photographs of her paintings. I tell my son to switch on the light,
switch off the light. This illuminates *El Primer Encuentro*

another rendition of the meeting that ignited the first
transcontinental disaster

my son's first encounter
with unfair exchanges:

jade & watermelons
for gunpowder & extinction.

He puts his tiny finger on the switch
for change, one needs a single finger, I tell him, though I don't

say the part about power or how a small action by a single man alters natural
progression, yanks a chain link from a heart or a rough estimate of 53-million

hearts. When my son leaves,
I still hear his cries. Like the time I heard La Llorona's phantom pain

dribbling on neighborhood sidewalks. The first woman to choose
drowning her children by her own hands. One imagines choices:

dignified brevity over
prolonged disfiguration of the self, of the soul.

The first time Cihuacōātl saw the future
of her children, she cried every night drenched

in the impotence of running in water.
Outside, the wind shakes the jacarandas

& I see the first time I climbed a tree
the first time I bit into a fig's velvet skin
the first time I birthed a child, my bloody body
limp & full
of ecstasy. My son flicks the switch on and off
Aurora's round cheeks & humble smile
shine & disappear at the whim of his hand.

The Female Protagonist Deports Herself for Love

yo soy mexicana vengo a que me deporten
la Gaviota says. the bird is
without wings
without a boarding pass
that will take her, handcuffed
to her lover
who is kissing
another as we speak.
gaviota crosses
herself & and the atlantic
please virgencita let me
make it back to him

Cellular Memory

The monarch migration always reminds me

>   we placed her body in the ground
>   wrapped in plastic meant for vegetables.

Three priests from her birth town refused to come
out of the temple & sell us a blessing.

>   She would have loved to be buried in her raw silk
>   yellow suit & roses in her hair to match.

She would have sung

>   like she did on her last birthday, *fallaste corazón,*
>   shooting my grandfather irreverent stares, a belated attempt

at retaliation. Each year monarchs remember
to fly from Canada to Michoacán. Most of them die

>   on the way & their children take the lead
>   though they've never made the trek.

They know where to turn. It's always
the grandchildren on the way back

>   every September that pass through Texas.
>   When I watch the swirl of colors

I'm back in the car headed home
to Texas from Zacatecas after her funeral

>   stuck in the backseat watching the Joshua trees'
>   yellow blades amongst red dirt. As a child I always imagined

they were ballerinas. My mother & brother,
pilot & co planted in their seats like succulents

>   a silence only interrupted by the song
>   of fracturing wings

Receta de Enchiladas Rojas

Looking for my Abue's enchilada recipe
I found a lacquered bookmark,
1946-2020 Carolina Ramirez Martinez
Life marked by arithmetic
a simple subtraction
one plus grief is less than
one year without seeing

her in a cargo-less train
stuck with a calcified scenery
saying *el día que dios me ocupe*
estoy a su servicio
But the whistle corrects
Tengo miedo
no dejen que me entuben

I don't believe in stars

but she was a pisces
like me. Except she
tilled sadness with a comb
each morning taming
her curls. I want her
to be the white cloud minnows
sparkling at the dentist's office

& not disintegrating
amongst dirt, *el hoyo donde*
te dejará Jehová si no te arrepientes
y regresas a Él, like her mother
often warned

I'm terrified y desesperada
por escuchar su voz
in the last voicemails
she left. *Reportese, Lindita*
¿Cómo está, porque no me contesta?
en las parrandas

Yo, la paloma negra,

The bookmark reminds me
saying goodbye doesn't mean
we won't see
each other
I should swallow
all the platitudes
invented for death like   I swallowed

chlorine water, hit my head
on the concrete, sunk
in all that blue, content
with my end

A man in cowboy boots dove
in & pulled me out
I was eight. I lost two teeth & my   fear of death

                                        Abuelisa, ¿le tiene miedo
                                        a la muerte?
                                        No Lindita. ¿Qué sentía antes de nacer?

Nada, Abue. Nade, Abuelisa, en un lugar
donde la sal del mar besa al agua
dulce. ¿Se acuerda? Como flotabamos juntas
en Bacalar. She wasn't used to traveling without
her husband supervising. I understood why
she was so afraid of the clear water
even when her feet touched the sand

I understood why she never gave Abuelito
that letter we found in a pocket-sized, cheap spiral
bound notebook. Did she mean for it to be found?

                                        No dije nada. Me hice pendeja
                                        Me trataste como una cucaracha

I never heard her curse
but here she'd written *Pendeja*
in her elegant cursive

She must be on the balcony,
where tía Coco said she spent hours
unable to speak, reproaching her husband
her hair uncombed. She watched people
in the street in her chiffon-coffee-stained
blouse & a Caguama under her chair

I gather four wide guajillos,
watch the seeds
of chiles de árbol
settle in the sink. Smash a wheel
de chocolate Abuelita, seemingly
indestructible. I chuck a chopped
onion. It's so sweet, that movement of
inanimate things. The bouncing in the
hot oil. All they need is heat

I am missing something

I reach for my phone
before I remember, I must
work from memory

Sleepwalking Ballad for Ezequiel Hernández Jr.

My brain is a night bloom, a jasmine. She begs me
to think until I reach that place & I can't return

like a moth swallowed
by an evening primrose

I say this to you
before turning out the light.

On the way to our Airbnb I read about
Ezequiel Hernández who was killed just a few miles from us.

A marine shot him while he herded his cattle
mistaking an 18-year-old for a terrorist.

I'm trying to stop this now. I'm trying not to ruin
our first night of vacation.

But the loud desert winds remind me
I am untethered, afraid of spinning out

my survival instincts too are often wrong.

Don't fear snakes, they only attack
when they determine a threat

I've bitten all my lovers. So I pray, hiding in mesquites
& blackbrush in thick leather boots.

It's April. The first week of rain here, maybe the only one this year.
Prickly pears bloom, the landscape explodes with color.

We're so lucky! You say. Ezequiel wasn't, I think of saying,
but I stay quiet. I'll stay positive like you. . .like that sweet

boy. I see him. He sleeps & when he wakes, drinks his mama's coffee,
kisses her cheek, tightens his belt, shakes his head,

smiles at her usual despedida full of concern
be careful, she says.

He crosses beneath Mexican Persimmons, parts
the Sandsage brush, then gazes at the horizon,

everyone knows he loves landscapes & keeps
a drawing pad on him at all times to capture

so much vast sky that could swallow him

& it does. He rides a gentle beast, alert for thorny
mesquites. His eyes suddenly full

of the kind of worry only good men
carry, men who'd die for their family

& he will
get off his horse blinded by daybreak

lights. I say this to you but you're already asleep
you're already in another world.

Heaven

There is Heaven Of Course

       my mother
her name is another pretty   word for the sublime
               sometimes i close my eyes
    & spell out   H-E-A-V-E-N

  in blue   letters   especially when i look out   of windows when i can't fall
asleep   Heaven is father

  & mother   no time for childish wishes   or toys *no tenemos dinero*

she rises   with the sun   puts on creased boots   mascara   brushes her hair
      into a ponytail
grips me between her thighs   pulls & tugs

      my hair sliding the comb's tail through my scalp
i cry quietly before ripping out   the clips   my braids unravel

Heaven   is already in the cold   street entering
      the alleyway lined with colorful tarps   vendors arrange the day's goods

i watch swirling glass marbles   refract sunlight   on the wall
     pink & black fish glimmering   in plastic   bags swinging in the air

                eight-foot chinese roots & rubber stingrays

     a man balances a wooden stick over his shoulders
pendulum buckets filled with guayabas & higos   lady justice   *guayabitas*

frescas baratas andele andele animese

I'm a Small Child Heaven Carries

like a purse she stows me under   the faux granite counters   *be quiet* strange request

considering the tongue-clicking metal beast behind us

Heaven picks up a sack of maize   she slits the bag & dumps the teeth

        into a boiling pool foaming yellow   Abuelisa & tíos all reserve these jobs for young

men   Heaven's only helpers are her two hands   she folds up wax paper & turns it

into a torch   tossing it into the belly of the machine   while the beast heats   Heaven

rolls masa into white spheres   sometimes she stops to help a customer & while she is

distracted i slam my body against the thick masa   unbudging clouds   *are they glued ma*

or just really heavy? Heaven ignores me & lifts the sphere over her head

with both hands like atlas   the world on her shoulders   she slides two wide cutters

inside the beast's mouth   soon freckled circles puff up like globe fish then fall onto a

wire net moving toward a basket where Heaven lifts them   we know tortillerias are

dangerous places   Heaven will fracture   bones & uphold her family's pride by

being self-sustaining   self-mutilating   *Heaven i'm bored*   Heaven is irritated

el aburrimiento es para la gente rica y floja go sell this cheesecake   when the sun falls

Heaven dives   belly first on the bed *baby can you give me a foot massage like last time's*

        i rub vaseline & talcum powder on her calluses

once the lights are out her crying fills the cold room her feet shining in the dark

        her hair covered with a muslin of stars

Please Stop Behaving Like a Desperate Dysmorphic Sex Beast

today Heaven is happier   than usual   she rose at seven in the morning on a sunday

she mops the cracked   mustard linoleum floors & we sing Alaska & Diorama's

       la gente me señala me apunta con el dedo

Heaven is radical by modern   standards but here the Colonial Oppression Preservation

(COP)   send her a notice in the mail *if you'd like to avoid   a*

        loose   woman

tariff please stop   behaving like a desperate   dysmorphic sex beast. In the meantime,

cut the enclosed   red A following   the dotted lines with small   scissors.

Carefully peel   the back of the sticker   and press it onto   the backside

      of your voter's license.   We'll be in touch soon.   Thank you.

      a man left us   then another

she is migajas   de los hombres esta *loca*   ironically these indictments

make her   full of rage

      she sends a letter back   using words she learned   while getting a science

    degree   she often gloats about in conversations   an educated

woman

another impuesto to pay   her macho father & my sweet loving   father

figure loves   her to death   offers help   she says no   she wants to prove

something   so we listen to women   sing about   rebellion

     a quién le importa   lo que yo haga

    the telephone rings   *we are cutting off power*

the lights go out & we stop   dancing

i can tell she's holding back   tears i tell her not to worry   we have all   we need

food is everywhere   you look   on sidewalks   & at Abuelito's house

she stays   quiet   kneels next to me

i'm so sorry baby this is all my fault

the next morning boxes arrive   toys clothes & this big red   jeep sent to us by a man

once   in our life who now   lives   in the Doghouse   Leonardo sends his love   in

the form of   cardboard   but we are not in   *need*   Heaven phones him *i need*

*your signature to take our child out of the country not your pendejeda*s   in the patio i ride

around in the jeep   waving goodbye at an invisible   audience   *adiossssssss*

          the clouds move   quickly above me

what will   drift   away next?

this will be the last   time   we have   our own home   though i was once

afraid   of its history   an old catholic   school   startled   by

noises   during   the day when i was   alone   the radio turned on

i heard steps   out in the hallway   it was mine to love   mine to fear

while Heaven   is no superstitious   woman   she believes   in the

haunting   another notice from COP slides   under the front   door

she picks me up   her eyes full   of little bright   strings a sun inside   her

vámonos de aquí

We Want to Say More But the TV and George Bush Jr. & the Ads Selling Xenophobia Starter Kits Interrupt Us

Heaven is always the white line chalk on clay and cinder
before a race before the cock of the gun signaling the start

before I could speak I slithered out of her scaled flesh
a little winged creature she thought when she saw me

what a pity non-collapsible bones flimsy wings
but the gods had chosen   she too was nothing   but blood and cartilage

wired by lighting memories of the women before her
carried inside her bitter grandmother bat-winged preaching with shiny dentures

over enunciating *Jehová* and had He already taken her away from the torture that was sex
without love sex without the only man she had wanted sex with sex as a transaction of
practicality sex as sacrifice for preservation hers and her family's

but how was my mother like her sacrificial   *entregada*   full of self perseverance this
thrashing passion of a mexican woman but I'm getting sidetracked

that's my concept only grasped after it was all over after   becoming other
you find pain is different   that mesozoic shell extracted by oil rigs and hydraulics
and injections of water and sand

a violent reach for the mother's core a dream of perforating the shale   and finding
a pearly egg

here in texas people come to find their fortune and we are no different except when
*Lin, don't be fooled   we are different   is it not amazing I was not a woman of color until we
crossed that line   it's true what they say
change comes like an early train*

*sí ma but do you think the change crawls   inside   from the outside or   crawls
outside   from the inside*

it crawls from where you   first spot it

and we want to say more but the sounds of the TV and its George Bush Jr. and bomb threats
and its photos of children playing in debris and its news of foreclosures and repossessions
before it cuts to late night ads of soldiers with robotic legs selling support our troops magnets
interrupt us

she turns it off with a finger *hora de dormir*

i want to ask her about her abuelo my great-grandfather and how he was known as el indio
back in Zacatecas and about his tales of riding around with General Pancho Villa *i don't
remember them* but Villa was kind of a maniac she tells me *sanguinario*

she prefers Zapata—*less explosions more intellectual propagandism but his heart was in the right place*

she wishes she'd listened to his stories and i wish she'd kiss me goodnight
braid my hair but she smells the blood between my legs

treating me like a child will only disservice me keep me weak
when she knows the world won't treat me like a child the world will exploit
my girlness now inside a woman's body here in this beige liminal space
of strip malls

where was i going with all of this? maybe toward connecting with you   or maybe
to heat a tar pit just enough until it gushes

a rush of unburying oneself

Two Women Capable of Sex

you look like a boy with that hair
Heaven's snake eyes linger on me
everything is a problem
the loud music
the studded belts
the boyfriend lingering after
dinner pushing her to finally
ask if he needs a ride *this late*
she can take him or are his parents
already on their way *you can wear*
yours like a girl i scoff and shut
the bathroom door
a wall of fissured oaks
this roughness exclusively built
for keeping women capable
of sex hating each other

at the dinner table of chiles rellenos
rice salad beans and a shared glass
coke *i want to go back*
you don't get to decide you're a child
we will when we build our house there
i want to tell her we *had* a home
in Abuelito and Abuelisa's house

but we stay silent until my little
brother circles the table flying
his little robot around
sit down we're eating

te pido que me [redacted] y ames tal cual

[redacted] podremos tener [redacted]

[redacted] ahora.

Quiza, [redacted]

[redacted]

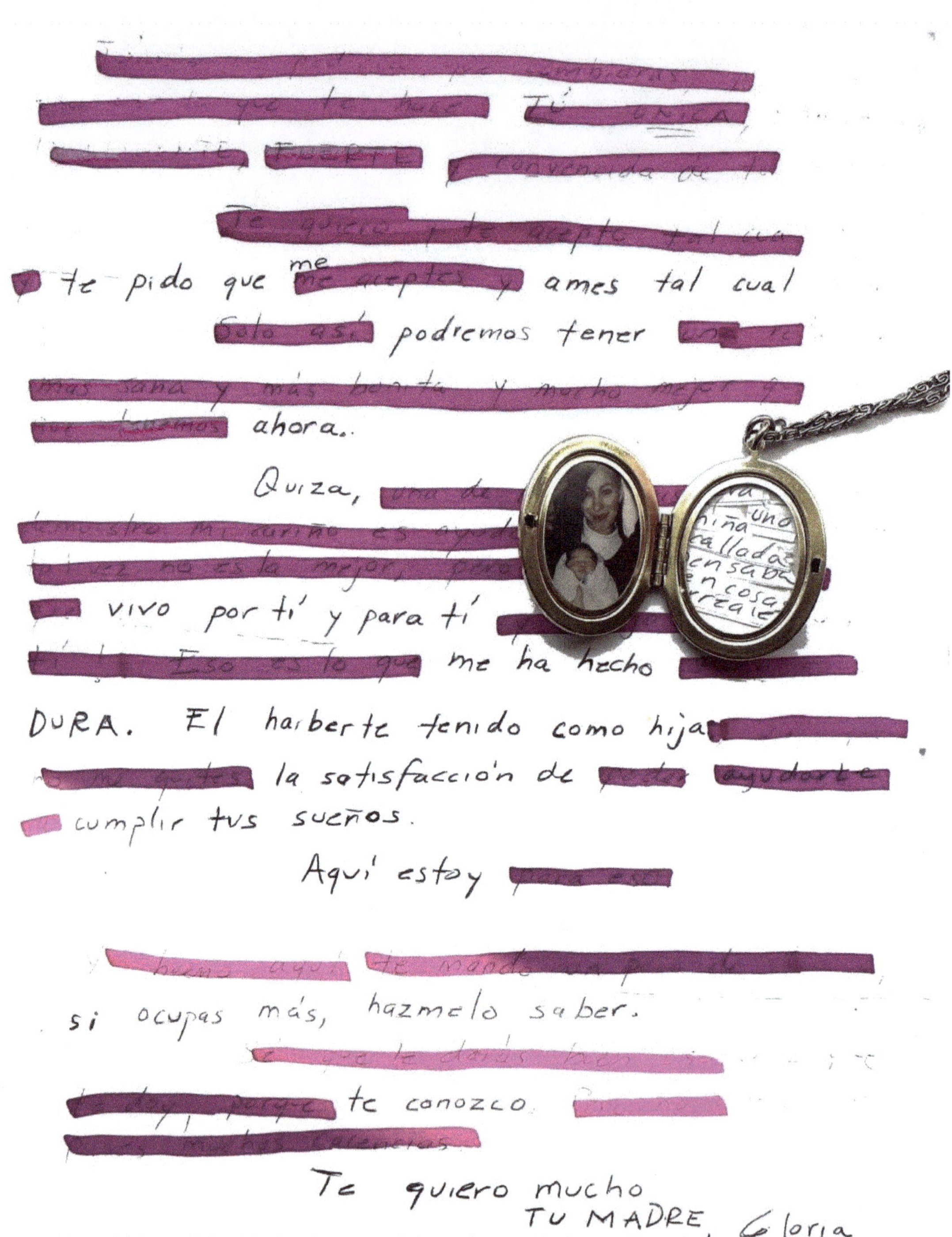

vivo por ti y para ti

[redacted] Eso es lo que me ha hecho

DURA. El haberte tenido como hija [redacted]

[redacted] la satisfacción de [redacted] ayudarte

cumplir tus sueños.

Aquí estoy [redacted]

[redacted]

si ocupas más, hazmelo saber.

[redacted]

[redacted] te conozco [redacted]

[redacted]

Te quiero mucho
TU MADRE, Gloria

Septiembre 25th

Hey linda!

Hoy pensé en ti. Hoy pensé en lo difícil
que la pasaste en tu niñez. Hoy pensé en ti y
en todo lo malo que pude haber hecho hacia tu
persona. Hoy pensé en ti y lloré...

Lloré por todo lo que pude evitar y
no lo hice. Lloré por todo lo que perdiste por
mis decisiones. Lloré porque no te hice feliz.

Hoy pensé en ti y quise hacertelo
saber. Hoy pensé en ti y en lo mucho que te
quiero. Hoy pensé en ti y también en lo
que te he fallado. Hoy pensé en ti y pensé
pedirte perdón. Ya sé que eso no cambia

el pasado, pero podría cambiar la manera
en como llevamos nuestra relación de aquí
para adelante.

Hoy pensé en ti y pensé en
decirte tantas cosas, que a veces hasta
olvido.

Hoy pensé en ti y quise
que te quiero como nadie te ha querido.
Hoy pensé en ti

no es forma deseada, pero
soy.

Hoy pensé en ti, y en cómo pueda
transmitirte mi amor, protección y ayuda
Sé que me he equivocado en muchas
cosas, pero eso no cambian todo, lo que siento
por ti ahora.

Me has hecho muy ___ a al
graduarte de tu escuela, el ___ y
carismática. Que no hay ___
cliente pregunte por ___
Me has hecho muy
___ aceptada en varias univer___
___ al que quizá no sentimos
nosotros, pero a pesar de todas sus imperfecciones
nos ha aceptado.

Lin, Hoy pensé en ti. Hoy
has publicado un 'LINK' en facebook
una publicación que quizá te cayó como
___ muchas personas, pero a mí TU MADRE
___ igual, te que seas, como seas ya te sigo
___ más aún por tener esa valentía
___ el mundo tal cual eres (cosa que yo
___ he podido hacer), AMO esa osadía que
___ luchar por tus sueños y convicciones

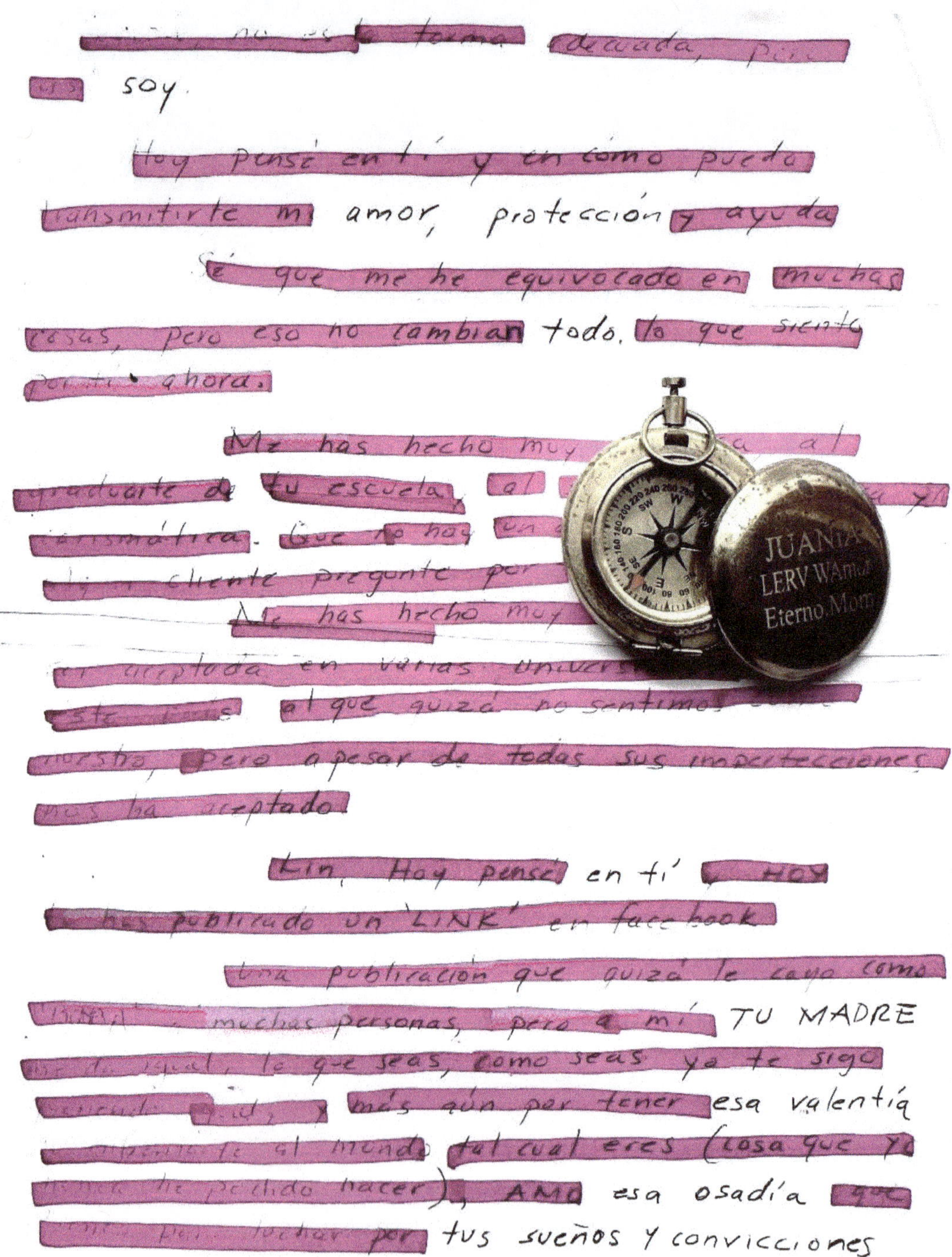

The Doghouse

HERE -
You are
black ink.
Alien
Other
lost,
error.
What is
Renewal
Family
(First

51

continued
(You must also answer
Care
Lookup)
the purpose of
your father's birth
your mother's birth
where you are
the space
entered

52

There are 11 million undocumented immigrants in the US

nearly half of us are Mexican. But before my family wound up stuck in the Doghouse, we had gone there temporarily and returned after a period of no more than a year with some savings that would get invested in town, plus back into the State's economy. We paid taxes with ITINs and spent money at the store. *Clarines*, we spent money everywhere in the States, buying things we never thought we could hold in our hands. Things, things, things, corrupting the soul. Driving us further and further away from our dreams.

> We migrated between the 1990 and 2006, coinciding with the statistic: "half of
> [8.5 million] those undocumented in 2011, arrived between 1995, and 2004."[4]
> This was also during the extreme militarization of the border like never before.
> The request for an operation,
> an excision, in El Paso,
> *Hold the Line*, said,
> Silvestre Reyes—formerly wild and formerly king
> in the Doghouse, he believed to be a grey wolf.
> Even though he used to share our bowl,
> twenty miles of the border unearthed cage
> after cage full of wolves ready to shoot.
> Then another plan. . .
> San Diego's 1994 Gatekeeper
> sprouted sixty miles of walls
> as if by a miracle
> deployed thousands of
> border patrol agents,
> stadium lightning, vehicles, sensors.
> We were entering
> the beast, we were on our way
> to becoming beasts ourselves.

---

[4]Aviva Chomsky, *Undocumented, How Immigration Became Illegal*

The Doghouse is Colorless, Odorless

devoid of sound stiff with muted browns identical houses   haunting symmetry
i can no longer sleep in the silence of night i don't believe other people live in
the surrounding houses
there are no children playing in the streets no late night backyard gatherings
there is only waking up in darkness traveling one hour to work
i sleep the entire ride leaving Heaven alone with her searching eyes on the
road it's easy to tell when she's planning she has that deep distant gaze she
hardly breaks out of her trances to sing a song on the radio or listen to the
news her eyes narrowed as if trying to squeeze an answer to her dreams
when we arrive she is kind enough to let me sleep in the empty back of the van
until it has to leave for the early deliveries
at the new tortilleria men trickle in before sunrise to reap their breakfast their
hair combed & smelling of aftershave
by lunch the men return tracking in dirt covered in sweat they hand me
dollars with starched hands always smiling
they carry a cheerfulness i see nowhere except here & it's a gift knowing they
worked long hours under the texan cruel sun

In the Doghouse I Am Rabid

& i the second in command   Heaven   alpha   she is not in my dream / nor is she on the roof / keeping watch she is elsewhere / she is out selling her coat / she is out killing / herself she is out to provide / as they say i am alpha now   all hail the queen / as a queen i am no woman / i am dictator / Heaven's cub now mine submits to me / he is afraid of tornadoes & hides / in the bathtub when the television goes blank / rumbles / a dead phone line sound / a hellish frequency / it terrifies me too but i don't let on / i comfort the cub when he is afraid / & when he wants to play i deliver blows / hardly physical but of beast / i am alone i am tired & the skin around my eyes is dry

Mystic Hostility

the wind whistles with hostility outside my apartment / i am tempted to think it's a message / mystic / so i go searching the Heavens / for a skylark & venus / the morning star / but their spirit doesn't come down / they're banished by metal wings / of military helicopters / in the Doghouse there are so many blades / cutting through the air / prohibiting the sublime / this may not be your experience / maybe i'm looking too much into it / maybe i'm wrong / but since i moved here / the nightmares won't stop / a wolf chases me carrying a rifle / smoke & screams follow / i am his next target / he knows of my usurpations / my dog body he detests *fold your hands over / your head get on the ground if he comes into our classroom do not fight / hide under your desk / your hands over your head /* but this is sixth period / in the ESL trailer / outside the real school building / & we're not scared of active shooters yet / but every once in a while / when the teacher is late or leaves the room / someone yells *¡la migra!* / we turn off the lights & hide / under our desks giggling / waiting for our joke's end

Ella es muy bonita y buena

on my way to work where i'm a shiny token, i flaunt a *huichol* choker / made by this *huichol* teenage girl in my hometown / a mother of two / large honey eyes / why did i walk with her across town / for a necklace? because in the Doghouse i find it rebellious to wear these / but mostly because i was lost   she invited me into her home / a room inside a blue-walled house with a big patio / *vecindades are fun on television. all the neighbors know & entertain each other / is it like that here?* she looked at me / she was now the one conceptualizing   her husband left to play his accordion across the country / they ran away together from their rancho /   i cannot remember her name only her cheerful eyes / my aunt called me a week later to say she'd hired a girl from out of town / *an india / she says she knows you & you're muy bonita y buena & asked for your number* / i'm almost to campus / when i slip down a mountain of grayish dirt / sprouted where the sidewalk used to be / *good afternoon may i pass through* i ask / a man with his face covered in a red bandana / we are matching   / i wear a red bandana wrapped around my hair / i speak spanish so he believes i'm kin / but i can't see if he's smiling / he looks confused / *no trabaje tanto tómese una chela* /   he remains silent he remains anonymous in the Doghouse / there are so many men covered in dirt the other men with him chuckle & return my *buenas tardes* / tardes tar stirring away in machinery i smile / say goodbye as if i'm boarding a ship

My Father Posthumously Weeps

quote why didn't you come see me

close quote

i haven't said it

deported deported deported deported deported departed de partida deportada deportado
deportados removed exiled banished whatever you do do not sign the voluntary removal
whatever you do don't run stop signs whatever you do not open the door ask for a warrant
whatever you do remain silent

remain silent

remain silent

remain

      i said your name hija i asked for you where is my lindita where is my lindita where

i know a'pa

i have not been deported i sold my soul to the Doghouse it's not as bad as you think /
*you don't have to be always sniffing the shit / the Doghouse said it loud & clear we
don't want you / we hate the lot of you /* but he says none of this

he kisses my forehead a'pa lo extraño how are you here

i ask him to visit my dreams but when he has i've ignored him i've been too busy tending
to other Doghouse business

why am i still here? it's true what they say / you have heard them say it haven't you?
that we are different   our packs leave their own behind we leave our breeding grounds
& say we'll return but we know it's not true / we skin ourselves & walk around inside
out to resemble the gray wolf / i don't like asserting authority as if i know   / i want
to be independent though i wish to stop conflating independence with rebellion &
rebellion with self-destruction   can you offer solutions? i don't know who the
you is supposed to be

      i don't know if there is a you at all

      have i made you up?

      i wouldn't doubt that i've made you & the suffering

      it's hard to see yourself   without a mirror

The Devil Takes Me

my mouth is his vessel of course he is a man he is more powerful than my will & pills
       he is after the one I love   *blame it on your mother, hurt him like she hurt you* says the colonizer's head that's crawled out of the
garbage disposal *he has no right asking you to clean the sink remember his people killed yours*   all is not theoretical all is historical & God does not come   here   even when you pray   I flick my tongue continue my litany *the devil is here* I say but devil to my beloved is trauma is BPD I spit on his face to prove a point the wounded child learned from savages in her maternal bloodline   a grandmother who talked to spirits chewing tobacco between mezcales   if only the girl had access to the refined lineage of the negated father   the head recedes hiding in the plumbing I hear his whispers *you can't help but break everything you touch* ha! we both laugh

Abuelisa Caro

abue-lisa   i swapped the plosive *t* for a fricative *s*   a deflating balloon by the
untying of its tail is gentler than same balloon popped with a single needle /
appropriate for a woman like Abuelisa /abue—*lisa/ lisa* from the spanish
smooth / abuelisa foamed & flushed

      Abuelisa mi café Abuelisa mi avenita Abuelisa mi café Abuelisa mi avenita
      inverse reversed roles

i made up those verses for her and sang them every night while she bent over the
stove stirring a spoon in a pot of milk to harness its skin for me   we dressed sliced
french bread with white leathery nata   i hear this crunching and women
exasperated with joy or despair on the television screen i hold her manos in mine
drenched in blue light her manos a ripple of water a pleated crude satin

Abuelisa i pray each night for a visitation / for your warmth in my dreams / yet i've
seen you there only once / looking to buy a piece of mind / dainty button blouses &
over-the-knee pencil skirts / one store has it all / shelves laden with silks / gold beads
reflecting threaded gladiolas in your eyes / they glint & pierce through your *sed* / *seda*
embellished with paradises / is that where you are? / your hand sails the racks of
treasures / as if to make sure they're real / *pregunte lindita a cuanto cuesta* / you turn
to me / your yearning eyes ask for more / than translation / more than a favor / they
ask for clarity/ they ask where are we / really? but you're already dead Abuelisa /
ya no necesita *nada nada*

The Bureau of Premonitions

what are those flowers Heaven wants to know *del duraznero*   *peach flowers* it's
sunday Abuelisa died today around three o'clock a year ago   once i asked her
how a catholic school girl from the city felt the first time she rode on an old
motorcycle with a *pobre ranchero* how she felt standing in the orchard breathing out
for her to inhale its sweetness   i wonder if this memory was her last   i
pray her last breath wasn't clouded by the moaning bodies under white sheets in a
cold basement the doctor had called that friday *she won't do the exercises even
though we keep telling her they help by a long shot can you talk to her* he told my
uncle over the phone

can she hear music i asked *she is in such deep darkness she cannot even dream* what is a
body devoid of dreams

Yolanda Lopez died today peacefully with many of her friends   Abuelisa died
alone i tell my writing family my thoughts are fragmented now i'm unable to feel
anything other than anger & self pity   i read an article about John Baker's
theories of death by fear   he managed enough proof including airplane accidents
& formed a british government agency   the bureau of premonitions   Hmong
refugees died shortly after moving to the states from Laos   *dab tsog* ghost
pressing body how many immigrants have suffered a spiritual death to their dreams
of utopia only to be consumed by commodities racism & individualistic norms
    Heaven said *my mother died of fright* i've been unable to sleep haunted by sounds of
monarchs migrating crashing into windshields   i text my brother i love
you   how long do ghosts ride on one's chest

El tren de la muerte

or the beast is boarded / by about 500,000 per year /1,450 miles of horror / rape /
mutilation / we keep falling off the wagons / falling off monsters / birthed by governments
/ i say we but what i really mean

is i've tried telling this story so many times

i've stared out the window since 9:58 / this morning until the train / shook me from
my trance / i could see through its dirt-red aluminum / walls sounding like it's carrying
loose / forks & knives spoons & women weeping / Heaven weeping / my tía weeping / my
Abuelisa weeping / we suffer differently though / you'd thought i only inherited the vivid
colors but we know brightness / music dancing is mere consolation / for synchronized
historical tragedy / my beloved once told me / he saw a boy die of sadness / in Guatemala
after the boy's father / left for the Doghouse / he had never heard of that / but i'm well-
versed / we could die by watching a record / skip over the same missed / days like when
Heaven calls / to inform me this is mere / laziness my gripping memory by the arm / i'm
inclined to agree with her / she is usually right / a pragmatist

1. ***how suicidal are you? look at the chart*** / do you need to be driven to
    a hospital? where is your husband? the psychiatrist asks / i don't know i say
    laconically / i avoid giving her long answers since she's told me before she is
    not my therapist / she goes on about doubling my lamotrigine or prescribing
    more seroquel or changing me to lithium / she wants me to eat whole wheat
    bread she is very adamant about this / i nod diligently / the problem is i
    have always been a little slow at things i should be fast at / i spend so much
    time clutching words like skeleton / when i was a little girl & i wanted an
    aquarium i wanted my room to be an aquarium i thought the glass & the
    water & the fish would make a good shield / the fish were orange & blue &
    dotted & lined & they made me happy / i told Heaven i want a fish tank &
    she said no / i told Heaven i wanted sunday to be every day because it has
    the sun inside of it & she said no / i told me i wanted monday to be every
    day because it has the moon inside of it & i said no / we once mimicked
    each other's loneliness shared so much yearning & sidewalk adventures
    wailing every time a parent leaves & taking money for the small town arcade
    / tossing pesos away all day long being yelled at later that was supposed to
    be for la leche not for games & lots of smiling needing everyone to like you

2. femininity soothes me isn't it sweet to be looked at the way people look at the
    night sky for planets   masculinity grants me a place or a seat as they say
    it proves authority i become aggressive when they question my movement
    in the world like a dog becomes rabid when petted in a vulnerable place like
    a saber-toothed tiger i'm all two-edged knife all tooth & all extinct existing
    only through other people's depictions of me based on interactions frozen
    in time a caterpillar in my eye at a funeral of my parent's sibling my body
    a temporary blindness i choose again & again the stormburst blooming out
    of season the burden i place on the flower a memory then an abstraction
    like resilience mostly when it's on the roadside or in a vacant lot road a
    conjugation i must repeat until it's embedded in me & i am new she was
    resilient they were resilient i was resilient

3. at the grocery's pet aisle i look at the beta fish / one isn't moving at all / she
    is dead & she has been dead / i know this because of the moss flaking like
    contaminated radioactive snow / inside the five-inch diameter container / i
    cry until i am escorted out / of the store by an old man with a gentle voice
    / it will all be okay you see he points to the white / hairs on his head i didn't
    get these for nothing / i wait for my hair to grow back a frosty white / when
    this sadness petrifies me / i imagine me as a fish living inside a cave / where
    the sun slips in through a small crack / atop my home is where the water

is the bluest / a blue achieved only con agua y luz de sol / oxygen seeps into
my fish lungs & the sun warms my tiny fins / i hear Heaven remember that it is
easier to climb up on a downward slope than to climb down a downward slope

4. it's been decided that i will not keep on living in pain / i write pick up my
    lamotrigine at three / since i know i am one to forget / on the way i pray for
    a car crash / what would Heaven say / i hum the song she often quotes like a
    fable about a man who didn't listen to his mother who told him not to go out &
    he was murdered / when they brought her his body she asked to be left alone
    with him / dicen los que se asomaron que su madre, muy valiente, le dio de
    azotes al cuerpo disque por desobediente

Spiraling

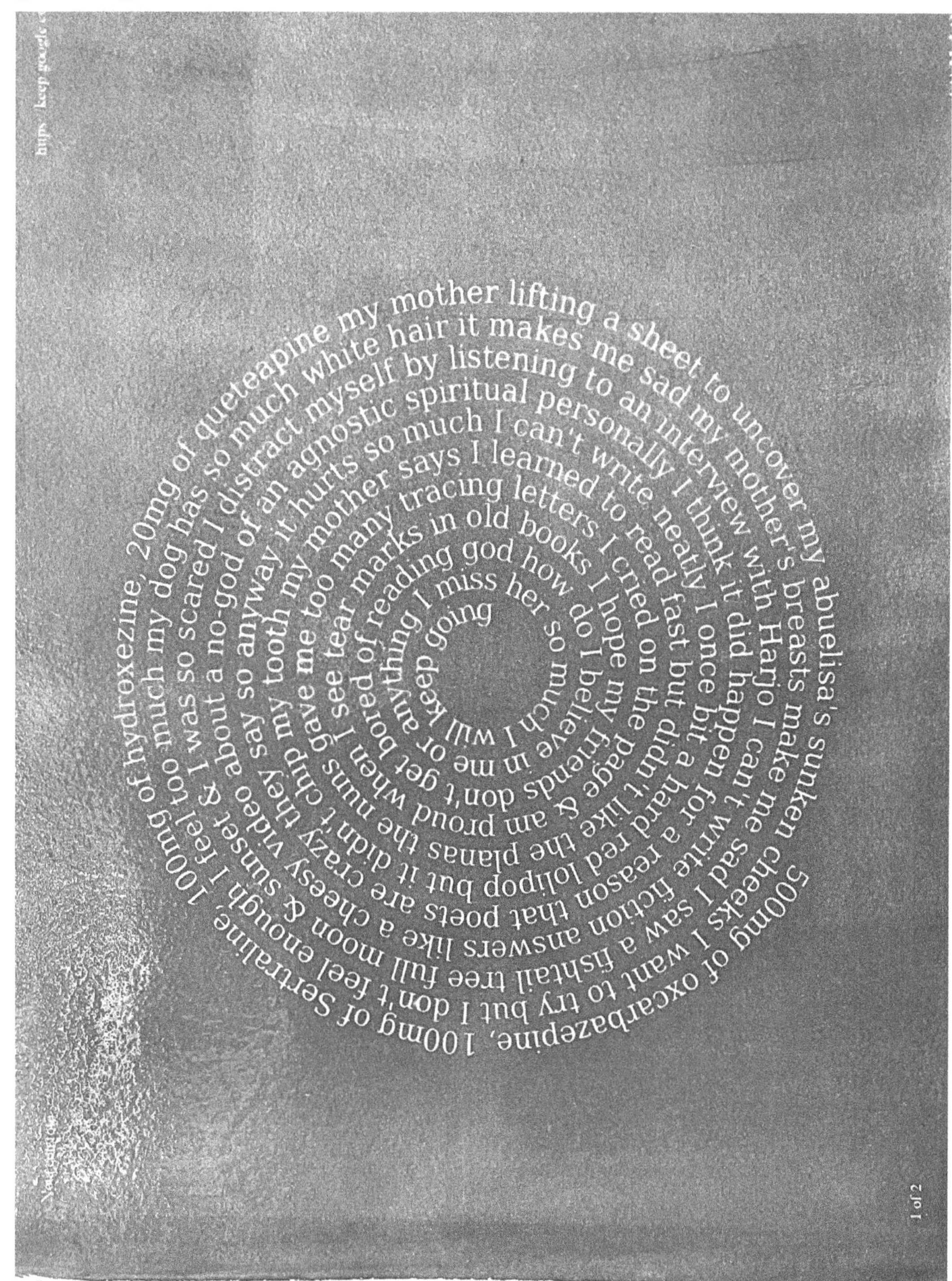

The Temple of Teotihuacán

I fill up the bathtub & make sure to add enough bubbles
so I don't have to see my body. Period blood clouds
the water & I think about how blood means love
in my language. I think about how where I come from
blood pleased gods. My therapist says *for you, love has to be extreme.*

What does it mean when you are bitten by a tarantula
& instead of getting help, you leave a wedding with the ex who

                                                strangled
                                                you
                                                two times
                                          he said

                            you know we belong together, Lin

                                                & the
                                                heavens
                                                opened up

my new beloved delivers sad news; he will not be
abused by me any longer. I buy all the books that will teach me
how to break the curse a difficult venom extraction for the uninsured

I've seen six therapists, two psychiatrists, a life coach, a pastor
& a witch. I am on all the generics my policy covers

Tomorrow I will dye
my hair neon blood.

                                  Will the world end before I fix myself?

The earth hurts & I with it. People migrate
sleep with frosted fingers, get bitten
& I write poems.   *Survival is resistance*, my beloved says
I know tomorrow   I will give
birth

                      to a little morning star.

PERMANENT
ELVIS VAZ
06 MAR 1995
they're dead or not really me
37 ● they're dead or not really me / parts of my body feel like
86 ● I'm so ashamed / I've let people down in lots of ways.
117 ● I'm always on my guard for someone trying to harm me.
DSM-5
Have you ever been declared legally incompetent or confined in a mental
Have you ever lied to any U.S. government official to gain entry into the United States?
Have you ever been deported from the U.S.
Zacatecas.
ALVAREZ LOZANO.
FIRMA VAN AL MARGEN.
MAIZ Y FRIJOL

Acknowledgements

I'm so humbled by all of the talented chingonxs around me. The poets who've supported me along the way, Cloud Delfina Cardona, SG Huerta, Amber Isaac, Dee Lalo Garcia, Gazzmine Wilkins, chan krishna. I love you all, my beloved lunatics. The chingones in my family who've picked me up from the depths of self-destruction and have loved me unconditionally: my mother, OF COURSE! MY MOTHER! I could and likely will write a book about all you've done for me, ma. My tío Javier who's been my mirror since I can remember, our souls bound by the magic of highly sensitive people. My tía Alondra, the first Chicana in my life, that badass who directed us through the hells of bureaucracy, used her sharp wit and impressive methods of getting things done whatever means necessary without needing a single book. My tía Lucero who baptized me "Juania." My brother Leonardo who I adore and has never voiced anything but cariño and admiration for me. My spouse Jordan Buckley who has weathered tremendous storms and catastrophic episodes of my illnesses—who has loved me through it all, honoring the tenderness and patience modeled by my grandparents. My son, my gosh! My son! Artemio! Te amo, chiquito. My little walking poetry. Thank you Juana Guzmán Mata for encouraging me to be a true Dreamer! I'd like to thank my mentors and those who've fostered my writing: Dr. Sara A. Ramirez, Tom Grimes, Jacinto Jesus Cardona, Emmy Pérez, jo reyes boitel, Jorge Renaud, Tammy Gonzalez, Dr. Roemer, Laura Chopnick, Murphy Anne Carter. . . I'm so blessed to have these amazing humans. I could go on forever. Lastly, a million thank yous to la Dra. Chan who took care of me for eleven years. Thank you all. Seriously.

Thank you to the editors and journals where these poems were published:

The Westchester Review: "catch & release"

Nat. Brut: "Recipe for Enchiladas Rojas"

Acentos Review: "Departation"

The NY Quarterly Review: "I Changed My Name"

About the Author

Juania migrated to North Tejas from Zacatecas as she neared adolescence. She spent most of her life without legal status. In the twenty-one years since her arrival, she's witnessed the deportations of her most beloved family members and the radicalization of the country's Right. Abstractions and laws weren't confined to paper or television—they materialized and destroyed her household.

She's spent the majority of her adulthood advocating for other undocumented people, whether through organizing, writing, or simply resisting being crushed by the towering pillars of imperialism. Despite being told she couldn't attend college, she holds an MFA in Creative Writing and other boring credentials granted by institutions.

Juania is a co-founder and editor at *Infrarrealista Review*, where she connects with other marginalized Tejanx poets and creatives. Since 2021, she has collaborated with the Texas After Violence Project, teaching at the Travis County Jail and conducting interviews.

Juania has struggled with severe mental illness since childhood and credits her survival to her grandparents, Arsenio Vázquez Muñoz and Carolina Martínez Ramírez—her guiding stars, who often shine their wisdom through her badass mom, Gloria Vázquez Martínez.